THE ART OF
THE COMIC STRIP

BY SHIRLEY GLUBOK

Designed by Gerard Nook

MACMILLAN PUBLISHING CO., INC., New York

COLLIER MACMILLAN PUBLISHERS, London

The author gratefully acknowledges the assistance of:

Alfred Andriola; *Milton Caniff*; *Frances L. Charman*, Curator, Historical Society of Buster Brown; *Harry M. Detjen*, President, Metropolitan Sunday Newspapers, and the Metro Staff; *Alison Dodd*; *Harry E. Elmlark*, President, Washington Star Syndicate; *Henry Geldzhaler*, Commissioner of Cultural Affairs for the City of New York; *Charles Green*, Curator, Museum of Cartoon Art; *Selby Kelly*; *Charles T. Kline*, President, Newspaper Comics Council; *Peter C. Marzio*, Director, Corcoran Gallery of Art; *John A. Pope, Jr.*; *Michael Pope*; *Bernard Reilly*, Curator of Historical Prints, Library of Congress; *Edward Summer*; *Alfred Tamarin*; *Brian Walker*, Curator, Museum of Cartoon Art; *Arthur Wood*; *Sheryl Glubok*, *Leo Jakobson* and *Lauren Nook*, junior advisers; and especially the helpful cooperation of *Avonne E. Keller* and The Newspaper Comics Council

Thanks to the following for permission to use material from their collections:
Alfred Andriola; Milton Caniff; Historical Society of Buster Brown, New York City; Selby Kelly; King Features Syndicate; Library of Congress; Museum of Cartoon Art, Portchester, Connecticut; Ray Winsor Moniz; Newspaper Comics Council; Smithsonian Institution Division of Graphic Arts; The Swann Collection at the Library of Congress; The Arthur Wood Collection

Binding illustration: 1967, ©Walt Kelly, by permission of Selby Kelly, executrix

Macmillan Publishing Co., Inc., 866 Third Avenue, New York, N.Y. 10022
Collier Macmillan Canada, Ltd.
Printed in the United States of America

10 9 8 7 6 5 4 3 2 1

Library of Congress Cataloging in Publication Data
Glubok, Shirley.   The art of the comic strip.
Summary: Explores newspaper comic strip art from the 1890's to the present.
1. Comic books, strips, etc.—United States—History—Juvenile literature.
[1. Cartoons and comics—History]   I. Title.
PN6725.G57   741.5'973   78-24342   ISBN 0-02-736500-X

The comic strip is an original art form that started in America and spread all over the world. Newspaper comics were born almost one hundred years ago when newspaper publishers began to print cartoons, or humorous drawings, in order to attract readers to their papers. In 1895 the *New York World,* published by Joseph Pulitzer, featured a cartoon called "Down in Hogan's Alley," by Richard F. Outcault. All of the action was shown within a single picture, which took up a full page.

One of the characters was a smiling, barefoot, bald-headed youngster with large ears and just two teeth. He wore a long white nightshirt. Words that he would be speaking were written on his shirt. When printers wanted to experiment with a new yellow ink, they tested it on the youngster's nightshirt. This splash of color attracted everyone's eye. Soon people were buying the newspaper to see what the "Yellow Kid," as the child came to be called, was doing. The circulation of the *World* zoomed. Then William Randolph Hearst, who published *The New York Journal,* hired Outcault away from Pulitzer to do "The Yellow Kid" for the Hearst paper. Pulitzer hired George Luks, who was to become an important American painter, to continue "Hogan's Alley," so there were two "Yellow Kids" in two rival newspapers.

1896, by permission of King Features Syndicate, Inc.

4

1904

One of the characters in "Hogan's Alley" was a bulldog that talked. The dog became a star called Tige in "Buster Brown," a comic strip feature created by Outcault for the Sunday *New York Herald.* A comic strip is a joke or story told in rows of pictures that are called panels or frames. The same characters appear regularly. The action is carried along by the pictures and by words spoken by the characters. These words are usually enclosed in "speech balloons" that seem to come from the speaker.

Buster Brown dresses in fancy clothes. The patent leather shoes with button straps that he and his sister, Mary Jane, wear were named for her and are still fashionable for girls.

Buster is a mischievous child who gets into trouble in each strip, but he ends up sharing with the readers a lesson he has learned and a resolve to act better. In most comic strip drawings, "frame lines" enclose a picture within a panel. But in the Sunday page at left, Buster's foot is outside one of the panels, and the figures of the dogs are drawn across two frames.

"Buster Brown" became so popular with newspaper readers that Outcault was hired away from the *Herald* by Hearst's *New York American.* The *Herald* continued the strip under its original title with another artist, so Outcault gave his new Buster Brown strip a different title each week.

1907, from the collection of Ray Winsor

The boy in "Little Nemo in Slumberland," by Winsor McCay, has fantastic dreams every night. His companions in his dream world are Flip the green dwarf, who smokes a cigar; Impy the jungle imp; Slivers, a man who speaks in pig Latin; and the beautiful daughter of the King of Slumberland. One night Nemo dreams that they climb a cliff and come upon wild lions. Impy tames the beasts by talking to them in jungle language and they ride off on the lions' backs. In another dream he and Slivers slide down a banister that goes up and down like a roller coaster and seems never to end. On still another night Nemo rides on the back of a circus elephant. His adventures always end with his falling out of bed or

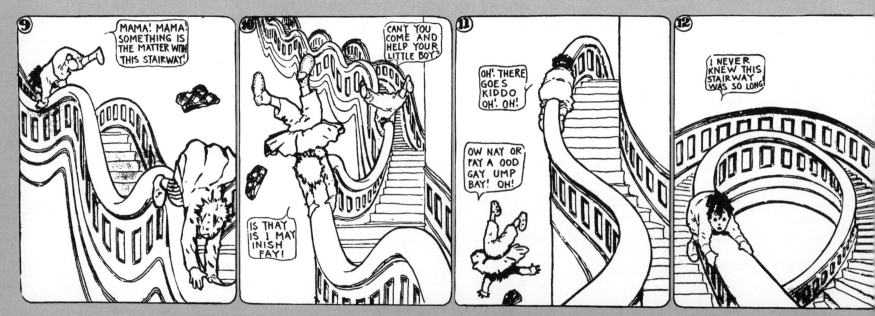

1909, from the collection of Ray Winsor Mc

1906, by permission of Ray Winsor Moniz

being awakened by his parents. The drawings in "Little Nemo" describe the action so well that few words are needed.

This strip is like a fairy tale; it does not tell a joke. Funny papers, or "funnies," as the comics section of the paper is called, do not have to make us laugh, but they do have to tell a story that can be understood quickly by young and old. Comics are supplied to newspapers all over the world by companies called syndicates, which also distribute news stories and other features.

1909, from the collection of Ray Winsor Moniz

Now here you go, Gran'pa---we'll soon teach you to ride.

Hold on tight, Gran'pa.

Oh, say, but what a tumble he'll take now!

Help, boys! Grandpa's going to fall off.

Oh, boys, I'm so afraid of falling!

Well, boys, I guess I've had enough for the first lesson.

Foxy Grandpa is a character who is always full of fun. The little boys play tricks on the old man, but he finds a way to outwit them every time. Grandpa has a large head, perhaps to show that he is wise. The artist moves the action along by placing the same characters in different positions in each of the six panels. In "Foxy Grandpa" the figures are large and clear and take up an entire frame; words spoken are printed under the frames. This strip was signed "Bunny," the nickname of Carl Schultze.

"The Kin-der-Kids" was signed "Your Uncle Feininger." The artist, Lyonel Feininger, who was born in the United States and then went to live in Germany, became famous as a painter. Feininger's drawings for the strip are in the style of storybook illustrations. Each frame has a different shape.

The Kin-der children are not happy at home with Aunt Jim-Jam and Cousin Gussie. The youngsters run away and take a trip around the world in a bathtub. Daniel Webster, the smartest of the Kin-der-Kids, is the navigator on the voyage, and his dog, a dachshund named Sherlock Bones, sometimes acts as a lookout. Pie-Mouth, who thinks of nothing but food, and Strenuous Teddy, a small boy who can lift enormous weights, are passengers. The children's bathtub, used as a boat, can go as fast as fifty-one miles an hour on the water. Runners put underneath the tub enable the children to travel over snow. Gussie and Jim-Jam chase after them in a rowboat and a huge gas balloon. Jim-Jam has a bottle of cod liver oil with her; as she pursues the children she tries to make them take their medicine.

1906, reprinted by permission of the Chicago Tribune-New York News Syndicate, Inc.

GUSSIE.   AUNT JIM-JAM.

DANIEL WEBSTER.

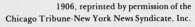

PIE-MOUTH.

Since 1897 Hans and Fritz have been getting into trouble with Mama and the Captain, a sailor who had been shipwrecked and rescued by Mama. The idea for a newspaper comic strip feature about the twins was based on an illustrated story about two mischievous boys that appeared in a humor paper in Germany. Hans and Fritz are supposed to sound as if they speak with a German accent, but they live in an imaginary land.

Hans and Fritz poke fun at absolutely everything and everybody. In the panels at left, the children have run off to play after Mama has told them about George Washington. They have heard that Washington could not tell a lie and that he was "first in war, first in peace and first in the hearts of his countrymen." As usual the boys will end up with a spanking.

Hans and Fritz first appeared in the *New York American* under the title "The Katzenjammer Kids," and were affectionately known as the "Katzies." Rudolph Dirks was the cartoonist. He wrote and drew the strip. Most comic strips are written and drawn by the same person. When a rival newspaper wanted to hire Dirks, he accepted the offer and took his characters with him. However, the name of "The Katzenjammer Kids" belonged to the first newspaper, which hired Harold Knerr to continue the strip. It is still running.

At the new paper, Dirks called his feature "Hans and Fritz." During World War I, when the United States was fighting against Germany, the title was changed from the German names of the children to "The Captain and the Kids." Rudolph's son, John Dirks, now draws this strip. Hans and Fritz are the oldest cartoon characters still appearing in the newspapers, but they continue to look like little boys.

"Reg'lar Fellers," by Gene Byrnes, is about neighborhood children who find ordinary things to do to amuse themselves. The gang includes Puddinhead Duffy and his little brother Pinhead. Byrnes used picture symbols that are popular in the comics. In the strip below, the movie usher's hat flies off his head because he is surprised. To show that some words are more important than others, Byrnes made the letters thicker.

Important symbols of the cartoonist's language were used by Bud Fisher in "Mutt and Jeff." In the first frame above, a series of dash lines leading from Mutt's eyes shows what he is looking at. A question mark over his head indicates amazement. To show surprise he falls backward, his hat flies off, his hair stands straight up and his coattails fly up. Marks known as speed lines follow his body as he runs. The stripes in Mutt's suit add to the feeling of motion. Fisher concentrated on the figures, with little background to distract the eye.

"Mutt and Jeff" is a "gag strip" that tells a different joke each day. Fisher first drew a feature about Mr. A. Mutt, who hoped to get rich by betting on horse races, for the sports pages of the *San Francisco Chronicle* in 1907. It was the first strip to be successful in a daily newspaper. Mutt, who is tall and thin, was soon joined by a short fellow in a high hat who called himself Jeff, after the world heavyweight boxing champion James Jeffries. When a rival newspaper hired Fisher away, he was able to take his characters and the title with him because he had copyrighted his own strip .

"Toonerville Folks," about a rickety trolley car in a small town, was created by Fontaine Fox in 1915, shortly after electric streetcars replaced horse-drawn trolleys. The Toonerville Trolley, which is always falling off the tracks, is run by an old man known as the Skipper. Little squiggly lines and circles and dots in the drawings give them a sense of jaunty madness.

In the topsy-turvy world of "Krazy Kat," by George Herriman, the cat, Krazy, is in love with the mouse, Ignatz; the dog, Offissa Pupp, is in love with the cat. The mouse hurls bricks at Krazy, and every time Krazy is hit by a brick she is happy because she thinks this means that Ignatz loves her. Offissa Pupp, who is a policeman, keeps arresting the mouse and throwing him into jail.

Herriman placed his characters in a mysterious desert with weird plants and trees and strange buildings. Backgrounds change; things appear and disappear for no reason; time switches from day to night and back again. The page is designed so that the frames create an overall pattern. Some of the panels are irregular in shape or size and have different kinds of borders.

The strip was written in a kind of mad poetry, with words spelled as they might sound. A Sunday feature told about the time long ago when mice had soft, shiny fur. One night when the sun went down and the world was dark, a visitor came from a distant land bearing a lighted candle. All through the night, the mice sat and gazed at the burning wick. The glow of the fire soon attracted hundreds of moths, which fluttered about the candle. When daylight came the mice discovered that the moths had fed on their fur, leaving them bare and bald forever.

1937, © King Features Syndicate, Inc.

The years between 1920 and 1930 sometimes are called the "Roaring Twenties." The agony of World War I was over. College boys wore raccoon coats and acted wild and silly. Women broke away from old social patterns. Many cut their hair, put on lipstick and shortened their skirts, and became known as "flappers."

John Held, Jr., created a newspaper strip called "Merely Margy" in which flappers appeared. Newspaper comics reflect current fashions in clothes, manners and speech and sometimes create styles themselves. Held's figures are drawn with thin, straight lines. Even the balloons have straight edges and square corners.

In the twenties women began to seek jobs outside the home, and working women appeared as heroines of newspaper strips. In order to interest women in reading the comics, Martin Branner showed "Winnie Winkle the Breadwinner" wearing a different dress every day, each in the latest fashion.

Winnie worked in an office to support her mother and father. She had a little brother, Perry Winkle, whose gang of pals was known as the Rinkeydinks. The words in "Winnie Winkle" take up almost as much space as the pictures. In the strip at right, Branner used a popular symbol of comic art — a group of stars to indicate a blow on the head.

Snookums, the baby boy of "The Newlyweds," is a brat. His parents, who call each other "lovey" and "dovey," are always trying to please him. Snookums took over the Newlywed household and the title of the strip was even changed to his name.

George McManus, the artist of "Snookums," also created "Bringing Up Father," which pokes fun at the newly rich. Jiggs, an Irish-born laborer, and his wife, Maggie, a washerwoman, suddenly become millionaires. Now that they are rich, Maggie acts snobbish, shows off and tries to make Jiggs take on fancy manners. Her home is filled with fine furniture and she wears stylish dresses and high-heeled shoes at all times. Jiggs wears a dark suit with a vest and spats, or buttoned ankle coverings which well-dressed gentlemen wore. The solid blacks of his suit give the pictures strength. McManus changes the positions of his characters' bodies and their arms, legs, feet and hands to show what they are feeling. Their wide-open mouths indicate surprise.

1921,
© King Features Syndicate, Inc.

Jiggs is not quite comfortable in his fancy clothes and he always is ready to take off his shoes. Maggie is constantly quarreling with Jiggs and keeps a rolling pin handy to throw at him.

"Bringing Up Father" has been translated into nearly thirty languages. Maggie and Jiggs have been drawn by several different artists, and they still appear in newspapers today.

1925, © King Features Syndicate, Inc.

For sixty years the daily lives of ordinary people in a small Midwestern town have been featured in "Gasoline Alley," created by Frank King. Walt Wallet, who owns a garage, is the hero. The strip began shortly after World War I, when the motor car had become popular. On Sunday mornings Walt and his friends liked to gather in the alley behind their homes and tinker with their cars.

One snowy winter morning, a baby boy was left in a basket on Walt's doorstep. Walt, a bachelor, adopted the child and named him Skeezix. Now and then a mysterious woman named Madame Octave appeared, claiming she was the boy's mother, and "Uncle" Walt had to go to court to keep him.

"Gasoline Alley" is a "story" or "continuity" strip, with a continuing narrative. It was the first feature in which the entire cast of characters aged year by year along with its readers. In the Sunday page at right, Skeezix is about five. The twelve panels are actually a single large picture with lines running through it to separate it into frames.

When World War II broke out, Skeezix joined the army. After the war he got married. Now he has children of his own, and the third generation of readers is following three generations of Wallets.

1930, reprinted by permission of the Chicago Tribune-New York News Syndicate, Inc.

The characters in "Moon Mullins," created by Frank Willard, are lovable but lazy. Moon lives in a boardinghouse where no one ever works. Often people with large homes which they could not afford to keep up took in roomers in order to meet expenses. Other boarders are Moon's little brother, Kayo, and Uncle Willie, who is the laziest of all. Kayo sees things as they really are and speaks his mind. Both brothers always look a little sloppy and wear bowler hats, indoors and out. In the panel below, from a daily strip of "Moon Mullins," Kayo is lying in the drawer that is his bed. The "z's" above his head show that he is fast asleep.

Barney Google's colt, Pony Boy, sometimes sleeps in a bed. Barney also owns a knock-kneed horse named Spark Plug and an ostrich called Rudy, both of which run in races. The cartoonist, Billy DeBeck, loved the sporting world of the racetrack and prizefight ring. "Barney Google" first appeared on the sports page of a newspaper.

1952, reprinted by permission of the Chicago Tribune-New York News Syndicate, Inc.

The lines in the drawings are loose, a style which suits the baggy trousers worn by Barney and his jockey, Sunshine. "Barney Google" was very popular. Certain

expressions from the strip, such as "heebie-jeebies," "hotsy-totsy," "fiddlin' around" and "time's a wastin'," were used by people all over America, and a song about Barney Google with the "goo-goo-googly eyes" became a hit tune.

In the 1930's Barney went into the backwoods of Kentucky and met the hillbillies Snuffy and Loweezy Smith. The Smiths became the main characters of the strip, which is now drawn by Fred Lasswell, and the title was changed to "Barney Google and Snuffy Smith."

Blondie Boopadoop was a flapper who worked as a secretary in the office of a billionaire railroad tycoon. Her boss's son, Dagwood Bumstead, liked Blondie. When his parents tried to prevent him from seeing her, he went on a hunger strike for twenty-eight days. When he married her, they disinherited him. The young couple settled down in an average suburb of a typical American city. In 1934 Blondie gave birth to a boy, whom they called Baby Dumpling. Seven years later his little sister, Cookie, was born. The children have been growing through the years and Baby Dumpling is now known by his real name, Alexander.

Dagwood provides the humor in "Blondie." Always late for work, he bumps into the postman and jumps onto a bus

that is already moving. His naps on the sofa and his relaxing baths are constantly interrupted by everyone in the neighborhood. In the middle of the night, he usually goes to the refrigerator to make himself an enormous sandwich. The "Dagwood sandwich" has become a part of American culture. Chic Young's drawings for "Blondie" are bold and simple. The attention is on the people; there is little detail in the background.

"Blondie" is one of the most widely circulated comic strips today. It appears in fifty countries in more than 1,500 newspapers and is read by 125 million people. It also has been made into movies and television programs. Comics have become an important part of our popular culture and influenced other art forms, including painting, ballet and theater.

A small girl about eight years old, named Nancy, has stayed the same age and size throughout the years. Her life and her surroundings do not change with the times. Nancy began appearing in the 1920's in a feature by Ernie Bushmiller named for her aunt, "Fritzi Ritz." Then she became the star and took over with her own name.

The figures in "Nancy" are drawn simply, with firm lines. A horizontal line represents the girl's nose; two round spots like buttons form her eyes. Her black hair looks like a helmet with a bow on top. The backgrounds are bare, and the contrast between the blacks and whites is strong. Most of the action is in the drawing; few words are needed for the gags in "Nancy."

The words are more important than the pictures in telling the story of "Barnaby," by Crockett Johnson. Barnaby is a five-year-old boy who has a fairy godfather named Mr. O'Malley. The fairy godfather has little wings and smokes a cigar, which he also uses as a magic wand.

Mr. O'Malley's magic usually ends up in confusion. For instance, he brought on a snowstorm so Barnaby could go sledding, but he did not know how to stop the blizzard and the snow got too deep for Barnaby to go out.

Mr. O'Malley does card tricks and likes to smoke Barnaby's father's cigars and eat whatever food he can find in the family refrigerator. Barnaby and his dog, Gorgon, are the only ones who can see Mr. O'Malley. He is supposed to take care of Barnaby, but usually the little boy has to take care of his godfather.

Johnson drew the figures in "Barnaby" almost entirely in outline, with no shading. The characters are seen from the same viewpoint in each panel, with little change in movement. The words spoken by the characters in this strip were printed in type set by a machine, rather than being lettered by hand. The small, even print gave the artist more room for the words, and the strip has the look of a storybook. Crockett Johnson wrote and illustrated children's books as well as comics. In some of them a little boy named Harold, who looks like Barnaby, is the hero.

"Henry," created by Carl Anderson, is about a little fellow with a bald, egg-shaped head, a long, thin neck and a potbelly. Henry never speaks and his expression never changes. He is quite clever and always comes out ahead. Since the 1930's Henry has worn the same short pants and tight shirt, in all weather.

In winter and summer a short, fat monarch with a pointed beard and square nose wears a long coat with an ermine collar. He always is shown with a crown on his head, even when he is sleeping or swimming. This pudgy little king does outrageous things that poke fun at ceremony. He has no name and he rules over a kingdom that has no name. His queen and their daughter also are nameless.

In fact, Otto Soglow, who created "The Little King," uses almost no words to tell his stories. When the queen speaks, a "tail" leads to her open mouth, but there is no balloon. The artwork in the strip is in simple lines. Everyone is shown in profile, or side view. Both Henry and the Little King first appeared in magazines before they were in newspapers.

Annie, a red-headed young orphan, constantly gets into trouble and has to be rescued by "Daddy" Warbucks, who adopted her. He is the richest man in the world. "Little Orphan Annie" is a continuity strip, with dangers lurking around every corner, creating suspense and making the reader wonder what will happen tomorrow.

Annie, who looks like a wooden doll, has acted the same and stayed about the same age for more than fifty years. When she was taken to live in the Warbucks home for a short time, Annie had some beautiful, fancy clothes. Since then she has continued to wear the same style of dress. She goes on saying, "leapin' lizards" and "gee whiskers." Sandy, her dog, just says, "arf."

Harold Gray, Annie's creator, started his career in comics doing the lettering for another cartoonist. When

Gray got his own idea for a strip, he wanted to call the child Andy. Captain Joseph Patterson, publisher of the New York *Daily News,* in which the strip first ran, changed the boy to a girl and called her Annie. In the thirties and forties, "Little Orphan Annie" became a popular radio serial with its own theme song. In the 1970's "Annie" was made into a musical comedy stage show.

"Wash Tubbs," another continuity strip, was created by Roy Crane. At first the short young hero was a grocery clerk, but soon he was running off to seek buried treasure and track down criminals all over the world. In the course of Tubbs's travels, he joined up with a square-jawed soldier of fortune named Captain Easy, who later took over as the hero of the story.

Crane's adventure stories and his fine artwork are equally important in his strips. To give the feeling of lively action, he might switch the viewpoint from one panel to the next. Sometimes the figures are shown close up or from a sharp angle, then from far away, then from the middle distance. This technique is common in the movies.

© 1935 by NEA SERVICE, INC.

1934, reprinted by permission of the Chicago Tribune-New York News Syndicate, Inc.

Terry Lee is the hero of an adventure strip created by Milton Caniff in 1934.

Terry's grandfather left him an abandoned gold mine on the coast of China. Terry and

his friend, a young man named Pat Ryan, set out to look for the mine and encountered

pirates, whose leader was the beautiful Dragon Lady. Three years after "Terry and

the Pirates" began, Japan invaded China and Caniff brought the war into the strip.

When the Japanese bombed Pearl Harbor, Hawaii, in 1941 and the United States entered

World War II, Terry joined the air force and became the pilot of a fighter plane on

194?, reprinted by permission of the Chicago Tribune-New York News Syndicate, Inc.

active duty in the Far East. People became more serious during the war, and the strip itself became more realistic.

Caniff draws his characters from different distances and angles, with a great variety of scenery in the background. He uses a good deal of shading and uses grays as well as black and white to add variety. Caniff balances story and pictures so they are of equal importance. In an adventure strip, both the words and the pictures carry the story forward. Each episode in "Terry and the Pirates" ends on a "cliff-hanger," as the note of suspense has come to be called, so that the reader will buy the next day's paper to see what happens.

This strip was copyrighted by a syndicate that owned the rights to the story and its characters. Caniff wanted to own his own strip, so he left that syndicate. George Wunder took over "Terry and the Pirates," and Caniff started a new adventure strip, "Steve Canyon," for a rival syndicate. This time he copyrighted the strip in his own name. Canyon was an air-force transport pilot in World War II and now goes to remote parts of the world on dangerous missions.

© Field Enterprises, Inc., 1978

A caveman named Alley Oop is the subject of an adventure strip created by Vincent T. Hamlin. Alley, who lives in the kingdom of Moo, rides around on Dinny the dinosaur, his faithful pet, and gets into scrapes with his prehistoric friends. He also travels back and forth to different places in different times with the aid of a time machine. Alley's strong body is drawn with straight lines and sharp angles. Hamlin changes the sizes of the frames to fit the pictures, and sometimes balloons extend beyond the frames.

"Tarzan" was based on the widely read novels by Edgar Rice Burroughs. The hero's parents were stranded, then killed, in the jungles of Africa, and their baby boy was nursed and protected by an ape mother. In time Tarzan became a powerful man who could swing through the treetops and fight off his enemies with only a small knife as a weapon.

The figures in these drawings by Burne Hogarth are shown from different viewpoints to give the feeling of strenuous movement. Hogarth changes the width of the frames to fit the action. "Tarzan" is drawn in the style of an illustrated story with the text inside the frames. Conversation is in quotation marks. There are no speech balloons.

Tarzan
by Edgar Rice Burroughs

"WE ARE DOOMED," SOROS GROWLED. "I HAVE SEEN THE STRIPED DEATH ENTER THE ARENA WITH TEN MEN---AND KILL THEM ALL!"

THE GREAT BEAST LOOKED UNCERTAINLY ABOUT----- FIRST UP AT THE SHRIEKING AUDIENCE AND THEN ABOUT THE ARENA.

IMPULSIVELY, LURUL ROSE, STRIPPED HIS SHEATHED KNIFE FROM HIS BELT AND THREW IT TOWARD TARZAN.

AS THE WEAPON FELL AT HIS FEET, TARZAN CAST A FLEETING GLANCE TOWARD THE LOGES AND PICKED IT UP.

AS THE TIGER SPIED THE MEN, A HIDEOUS ROAR BURST FROM ITS LUNGS.

MOTIONING HIS COMPANIONS BEHIND HIM, TARZAN SLOWLY ADVANCED TOWARD THE STRIPED DEATH. AS THE GREAT BEAST CHARGED, THE SCREAMING CHALLENGE OF THE BULL APE MINGLED WITH SAVAGE ROAR OF THE TIGER.

HOGARTH 10/10

918

Our Story: WHEN THE MISTS OF DAWN LIFT, A SHIP DRAWS INTO THE STRONG-HOLD OF GUNNAR FREYSSON, AND ARMED WARRIORS DISEMBARK.

1956, © King Features Syndicate, Inc.

Harold Foster was the first artist to draw "Tarzan" for the newspapers, but he gave it up for a Sunday feature that he created himself, "Prince Valiant in the Days of King Arthur." The prince was first shown as a boy who became a squire and served Sir Gawain, a knight of the Round Table. Over the years Val grew up, married and now has four children.

Each Sunday feature starts with a short account of what happened before and ends with a forecast of what will happen the following week. Foster draws scenery with accuracy. He is also careful to show correctly the details of dress, arms and castles of the Middle Ages. Each panel is a beautiful picture in itself, with an interesting background. The story is told in a text so that the words do not interfere with the pictures. Most comic strips run in both daily and Sunday papers, but "Prince Valiant" has always been a Sunday feature only.

TO GUARANTEE PEACE THE EXILED KING KEEPS HIS MEN IN FIGHTING TRIM—AND AFTER HIS REGULAR MORNING LESSONS—

PRINCE VALIANT STARTS ON HIS PERILOUS MISSION, ALONE.

THROUGH THE TORTUOUS MAZE OF THE FENS HE THREADS HIS WAY—

TOWARDS THE MYSTERIOUS FIRE THAT BURNS WHERE NO HUMAN SOUL SHOULD BE.

A CHANGE OF WIND BRINGS THE COLD GRAY FOG IN FROM THE SEA.

SOON THE WHOLE WORLD SEEMS WRAPPED IN THE FOG'S EMBRACE.

VAL STILL PUSHES ONWARD IN THE DIRECTION HE THINKS IS RIGHT UNTIL DARKNESS FORCES A HALT AND THE PRESENCE OF DANGER—

MAKES A FIRE NECESSARY.

3-20

BUT FAR OUT IN THE QUAKING MARSHES ARE EYES THAT GLITTER ANGRILY AT VAL'S INTRUSION.

AND A HIDEOUS DESTROYER IS SENT TO DISCOURAGE THE VISITOR.

HAROLD R FOSTER

37

1934, by permission of Robert C. Dille, Carmel, California

"**B**uck Rogers in the 25th Century," which takes place in the future, was based on a magazine story by Phil Nowlan. He began to write the strip for the newspapers in 1929 and Dick Calkins did the drawings.

Rogers, who had been in the air force in World War I, was working in an abandoned mine when he was overcome by strange gases which put him to sleep and preserved him in suspended animation for five hundred years. When he woke up, the year was 2430 and North America had been overrun by super-scientists from Asia.

Buck met Wilma Deering and they ride about in rocket ships and wear flying-belts which enable them to hop over mountains and rivers. They fight enemies from other planets with paralysis guns and disintegrator rays which can destroy ships and airplanes. "Buck Rogers" forecast many scientific inventions: monorail trains, walkie-talkies, jet planes, spaceships and space suits and the atom bomb. It even forecast man's landing on the moon.

"Buck Rogers" was the first science fiction strip. "Flash Gordon," by Alex Raymond, followed. The action of this strip takes place on Mongo, a fictional planet whose inhabitants threaten to destroy the earth. Flash, his girl friend Dale Arden, and Dr. Hans Zarkov, a brilliant scientist, travel to Mongo by rocket ship. In the strip below, Raymond's figures are drawn masterfully and the sizes and shapes of the frames are varied to fit the scene. Much of the story is told by a text within the panels, but balloons also are used when the characters speak.

Mandrake the Magician, who has extraordinary powers and is able to control other people by hypnotizing them, was created by the writer Lee Falk. Mandrake has an assistant named Lothar who is the strongest man in the world. Phil Davis was the first artist to draw "Mandrake the Magician." The hero is dressed like a stage magician, with a top hat, a tailcoat and an opera cape. Speech balloons are in box-shaped frames and the story is told in few words, to give as much space as possible to the pictures.

Falk created another adventure strip, "The Phantom," about a mysterious, invincible crime-fighter who lives in an African jungle, in a cave shaped like a skull. He wears a tight

costume with a hood and mask. When he takes off this costume, he is an ordinary person named Kit Walker. But in this role he wears dark glasses and keeps his collar turned up and his hat pulled down, so his face is never seen.

The Phantom, who made his initial appearance in newspapers in 1936, was the first comics character to wear a superhero costume. Superman appeared in comic books two years later and then became the hero of a newspaper strip. The Phantom in his "skull cave" at left, below, was drawn by Wilson McCoy.

A realistic crime-fighter who is a city detective is the hero of a strip created by Alfred Andriola. "Kerry Drake" is drawn with clean, sharp lines, and the expressions on the characters' faces reveal their feelings.

In the daily strip above, short statements in the first and last frames tell what is happening. A "thought balloon," with curly outlines, shows what the child, who has been kidnaped and will be rescued by Drake, is thinking.

The most famous crime-fighter of all, Dick Tracy, first appeared in 1931 in *The Chicago Tribune*. During this period the citizens of Chicago were being victimized by gangsters, so this cops-and-robbers strip by Chester Gould was timely. In the first week of "Dick Tracy," the father of his girl friend, Tess Truehart, was killed by mobsters and she was kidnaped.

Tracy swore to avenge the murder and rescue his sweetheart. He uses scientific methods to solve crimes. Tracy is not a superhero; he makes mistakes and is sometimes shot, captured and beaten.

Al Capp poked fun at Dick Tracy by inventing Fearless Fosdick, a plainclothes detective who sometimes appeared in "Li'l Abner." The main characters in the strip are Abner Yokum, the handsome hero, his mammy and pappy and Daisy Mae. This folksy story about a hillbilly family is set in Dogpatch, in the backwoods in the South. "Li'l Abner" started in 1934 during the Great Depression, when almost everyone in America was poor. The Yokums were even poorer than most. They wear ragged clothes and they have no electricity or running water in their log cabin.

Capp invented the idea of Shmoos, happy little creatures that love to be eaten. They taste like steak when they are broiled and like chicken when fried. They multiply rapidly and lay eggs and milk in packages. Other creatures, Money Ha Has, lay money instead of eggs.

1939, by permission of Al Capp

"Li'l Abner" is a humorous strip, but some of the stories are continuing adventures that keep the reader in suspense. Each year, on Sadie Hawkins Day, there is a race in Dogpatch; any man caught in the race must marry the woman who catches him. After eighteen Sadie Hawkins Days, Daisy Mae finally caught and married Li'l Abner. Marryin' Sam, the preacher, performed the ceremony for $1.35.

There is great variety in the drawing in "Li'l Abner." The characters are shown from different angles, with bold outlines, and sometimes they are silhouetted against the background.

About 1946, by permission of Al Capp

1939, by permission of Al Capp

Popeye the one-eyed sailor is one of America's best-known cartoon characters. He was introduced into Elzie Segar's "Thimble Theatre," a strip about the Oyl family, when Castor Oyl hired Popeye to sail their ship. He soon became the star of the feature and Olive Oyl became his "Sweet Patootie." When Popeye eats his spinach, he becomes a superhero and can cough up bullets that are fired at him, dive out of a plane and land on his chin, or walk through walls. Popeye says, "Well, blow me down," and "I yam what I yam an' tha's all I yam." Another character, Wimpy, who is always mooching hamburgers, says, "I will gladly pay you Tuesday for a hamburger today," and "Let's you and him fight."

The words "goon" and "jeep" come from "Thimble Theatre" and have become a part of the English language. Goons are creatures that live in rocks on the moon. The Jeep is a strange, mysterious animal with the power to foretell the future. A motor vehicle that was first used in World War II was named after it.

The world's most famous mouse was born in animated films and then appeared in a comic strip created by Walt Disney and Ub Iwerks. Mickey and his girl friend, Minnie, are cheerful creatures with large ears; they wear oversized shoes and gloves with three fingers and a thumb. "Mickey Mouse" began in newspapers in 1930, just three years after Charles Lindbergh made the first solo flight across the Atlantic Ocean. Mickey decided that he too would become an aviator, and he built his own plane and learned to fly it.

Mickey Mouse is perhaps the most famous cartoon character in the world. In Italy he is known as Topolino and in Japan he is Miki Kuchi. Although Disney did not draw the strip, his name was signed to it until his death.

An artist who worked in the Disney studios, Walt Kelly, created "Pogo," a strip about a friendly little opossum. The setting for "Pogo" is the Okefenokee Swamp in Georgia. Kelly's elaborate drawings of nature make beautiful backgrounds for the characters. Albert the Alligator, who chews a cigar; Churchy La Femme, a turtle who is only concerned about himself; and Rackety Coon Chile, who calls everyone "Uncle," are friends of Pogo Possum and regularly appear in the strip. Topics in the news often were subjects for "Pogo," and Kelly sometimes poked fun at politicians.

The characters in Charles Schulz's "Peanuts" are neighborhood children who talk like grownups. "Peanuts" first ran in 1950 at a time when it had become popular to talk about

psychology, or the study of why people behave as they do. The plots are simple, usually

based on a conversation between two of the children, and deal mostly with their feelings.

The hero, Charlie Brown, stumbles over himself in his efforts to do what everyone else does,

but nothing works out right. He often jokes about his own failures and tries again. His dog,

a beagle named Snoopy, succeeds in almost everything. The girls in "Peanuts," especially

Lucy Van Pelt, give Charlie Brown a bad time. Lucy's little brother, Linus, is a deep

thinker, but he gets very upset when he loses his security blanket. He says, "Sucking your

thumb without a blanket is like eating a cone without ice cream."

There are no backgrounds in "Peanuts," just a few lines representing the surface on

which the characters walk. The figures have large, round heads, big mouths and small,

shapeless bodies.

Camp Swampy, an army camp, is the setting for "Beetle Bailey," by Mort Walker. When the feature began in 1950, Beetle was in college, but he was soon drafted into the army to serve in the Korean War. He is still a private after all these years, and still looking for ways to avoid work and outwit Sergeant Snorkel. Beetle's eyes always are hidden under his cap or helmet. All of the characters have oversized feet, which gives this style of drawing the name, "big foot" art.

The drawing in "Beetle Bailey" is simple and clear. In newspapers nowadays, comic strips are printed in a smaller size than they were in earlier times, because paper has become so expensive and the number of strips has increased. At one time Sunday features filled a whole large page; now they are often as small as a quarter of a page. So the pictures in today's strips have to be simple and can no longer be drawn with elaborate detail.

Gordo, the driver of an old tourist bus, is the most eligible bachelor in the Mexican village of Del Monte. Other residents of the town are the wealthy Widow Gonzales, who would like to marry him; Ponce de Leon; Pepito, Gordo's nephew; Señor Dog; Señor Pig;

Señor Owl; Popo the Rooster and Bug Rogers the hungry spider. Gus Arriola, the artist of "Gordo," signs the strips with names such as "Meth Oozla" to amuse the reader.

Arriola uses different-sized frames for the drawings and sometimes no frame at all. In the Sunday feature below, he creates a variety of designs with the simple forms of a century plant and the child's hat. His lettering is also unusual. The words are all in letters of different shapes and sizes; some run across the whole panel and some are outside the frames.

49

In the "Broom-Hilda" strip below, the word "bonk" is so large it takes up more space than the picture, and "zoom" is written into the speed lines of the heroine's broom. Words such as "bonk," "zoom," "plop," "wham," "pow," "vroom" and "zap" imitate natural sounds and indicate action. Many of these words were first used in the comics.

Broom-Hilda, a comic, cigar-smoking witch created by Russell Myers, lives in a spooky forest and travels around on her broom. The witchcraft she attempts usually backfires. She

1970, reprinted by permission of the Chicago Tribune-New York News Syndicate, Inc.

is looking for a husband and always puts on her beauty wart before going out. Broom-Hilda's solid black hat and cape form a strong contrast to the white background.

"B.C.," by Johnny Hart, centers on a group of characters in prehistoric times who did silly things much the same as people do today. The hero is a caveman. He and his friends mope around or bustle about doing pointless chores. Other characters include talking animals and plants, as well as a hairy fellow named Grog, and Don Juan who invented the comb. Characters in "B.C." also discover fire and invent the wheel.

WHAT ARE YOU DOING?

I'M DUSTING THE GROUND, ...IT'S FILTHY!

WHEN YOU'RE THROUGH WITH THAT, THE CREEK NEEDS WATERING.

Gag strips with wacky characters became even more popular in the 1970's. Dik Browne brought to the newspapers a funny person who is supposed to be a Viking. "Hägar the Horrible" is about a rumpled warrior who wears a horned hat and a skin over his shoulder. He goes off on raiding expeditions to get away from his nagging wife, Helga. Hägar has a friend named Lucky Eddie, a daughter named Honi and a son, Hamlet, who embarrasses his parents because he refuses to grow his hair long and likes to take baths. There are no backgrounds and no balloons in the strip below. The loosely drawn figures take up the whole frame.

WHAT ARE YOU LOOKING AT?

I NEVER SAW YOU WITHOUT YOUR HAT.

SO?

HOW DO YOU GET IT ON OVER YOUR HORNS?

DIK BROWNE

2-11

Newspaper comics go into nearly every home in America and to almost every country throughout the world. They represent the lives and dreams of people of all ages and kinds. Comics reflect the world we live in and they change as times change. It takes just a few minutes a day to read them, but they affect the way we think and act. The characters in the funny papers help us to see the drama in our lives, and the comedy as well. By reading them we can understand ourselves a little better and laugh at some of the things we do. And as Buster Brown says, "a good laugh is worth a good deal."

1967, © Walt Kelly, by permission
of Selby Kelly, executrix

52